SPORTS THROUGHOUT HISTORY™

The History of

BASEBALL

Diana Star Helmer and Thomas S. Owens

The Rosen Publishing Group's
PowerKids Press™
New York

Published in 2000 by The Rosen Publishing Group, Inc.
29 East 21st Street, New York, NY 10010

First Edition

Book Design: Michael de Guzman

Photo Credits: pp. 4, 8, 10, 18 © AP Wideworld Photos; p. 6 Corbis-Bettmann; p. 12 UPI/CORBIS-Bettmann; p. 15 © AP Wideworld Photos and CORBIS-Bettmann; p. 16 Agence France Presse/CORBIS-Bettmann; p. 20 © Rob Tringali Jr./Sports Chrome USA and CORBIS-Bettmann.

Helmer, Diana Star, 1962-
     The history of baseball / by Diana Star Helmer and Thomas S. Owens.
          p.   cm.—(Sports throughout history)
     Includes index.
     Summary: Provides an introduction to some of the key events in the development of the game that has become known as America's national pastime.
     ISBN 0-8239-5469-2
     1. Baseball—United States—History—Juvenile literature.   [1. Baseball—History.] I. Owens, Tom, 1960- . II. Title. III. Series: Helmer, Diana Star, 1962- Sports throughout history.
GV867.5.H45 1999
796.357'0973—dc21   99-12139
                                                                                                               CIP
                                                                                                               AC

Manufactured in the United States of America

Contents

Around the Bases

Baseball was not always played the way it is today. Settlers coming to America in the 1700s brought an old game they had played in England called rounders. Like baseball, rounders was played with a bat, a ball, and bases. There was no one to make official rules for rounders, though, so the rules often changed with every game. In later years, rounders would change into the game we know as baseball.

By 1886, when this picture of the New York Metropolitan Baseball Club was made, baseball had become more popular than rounders.

Baseball Is Born

People played rounders in America for over a hundred years. In 1845, a player named Alexander J. Cartwright changed the game. Cartwright said that instead of throwing the ball at a player to get him out, players should tag each other instead. He also decided how

big the fields should be and that pitchers could throw the ball overhand if they wanted. People liked the new rules so much that by the end of the 1860s, rounders had died out. Baseball was born.

Cartwright was a member of the New York Knickerbockers.

It Takes Two

The first **professional** baseball team, the Cincinnati Red Stockings, was formed in 1869. More professional teams were formed soon after. Teams joined **leagues** so they would have other teams to play against. The National League started in 1876. In 1900, the American League began. The two leagues decided that the best team from each league would play in a **championship** called the World Series. The first World Series was played in 1903.

◄ *The Cincinnati Red Stockings was the first team that paid its players for full-time work.*

Minor Leagues, Major Hopes

By 1903, teams that weren't in the National or American League were called **minor league** teams. These teams became places for **major league** teams to train their players. Major league teams send **scouts** to **amateur** games. If a scout finds good players there, the

team hires them. These beginners play on minor league teams. As players improve, they move to better minor league clubs, and finally to the major league team that hired them.

Players often spend years in the minor leagues before they make it to the majors. Some never play for a major league team.

Women Play Ball

At the beginning of World War II, many American men, including baseball players, joined the army. In 1943, the owner of the Chicago Cubs, Philip Wrigley, decided to start a women's league. It was called the All-American Girls Baseball League. The women's games were very popular, but when the war ended and the men came back, people thought women should be at home, not on the field. The last game of the AAGBL was played in 1954.

◀ *Teams like the Chicago Colleens played softball at first. Later they played hardball, like the men.*

All Together Now

At first, baseball was **segregated**. Major league teams only let whites play. Black players played on **Negro league** teams. A man named Branch Rickey knew that this was wrong. He hired an African American named Jackie Robinson to play for the Brooklyn Dodgers. At Robinson's first game in 1947, white fans and players cursed and threw things at him. Robinson didn't fight. He played. Robinson played so well that other teams began hiring black players, too.

Jackie Robinson is a hero to people everywhere. ▶

Baseball Grows

Early major league teams played in big cities because they were full of fans. When families began buying radios in the 1920s, people all over the country started to listen to baseball games. Even more people became fans when television became popular in the 1950s. The major leagues added ten teams between 1961 and 1977, and four more in the 1990s. Now people all across America have the chance to go and see their favorite team play.

◄ *The Florida Marlins were one of the four teams added in the 1990s. Here the team celebrates winning its first World Series.*

Strike!

As baseball became more popular, players started to make a lot of money. Even so, in 1994, major league players went on strike for more pay. This meant that they wouldn't play ball until they were paid more money. There was no World Series that year.

This game was played in August 1994, right before the strike. The strike canceled the World Series for the first time since 1904. ▷

Fans were upset. Players already made a lot of money, much more than most Americans did. Fans wondered if the players loved money more than baseball. After the strike, fewer fans came to professional games.

Different Ways to Win

Baseball **records** often stand unbroken for many years. In 1927, Babe Ruth hit 60 home runs in one season. No player hit more than that until 1961, when Roger Maris hit 61. That record held until 1998, when Chicago Cub Sammy Sosa hit 66 homers, and St. Louis Cardinal Mark McGwire hit 70. People love to see baseball players make history, but the real winners are the fans who love the game.

◀ *Babe Ruth, Mark McGwire, and Sammy Sosa are all baseball heroes.*

It's a Small World

   People don't just love watching baseball, they love playing it, too. In 1939, a man named Carl E. Stotz started a baseball league for boys, called Little League. Later, girls were allowed to play, too. Today, millions of boys and girls all around the world have fun playing baseball.

Web Sites:

Check out this Web site on baseball:
http://www.totalbaseball.com

Glossary

amateur (A-muh-chur) Someone who does something as a hobby but not as a job.

championship (CHAM-pee-un-ship) The last game of a season that decides which team is the best.

league (LEEG) A group of teams that play against each other in the same sport.

major league (MAY-jur LEEG) A group of the best teams in baseball that play against one another.

minor league (MY-nur LEEG) A group of teams that are not as good as major league teams.

Negro league (NEE-groh LEEG) A group of teams that only had African American players.

professional (pruh-FEH-shuh-nul) An athlete who gets paid to play a sport.

record (REH-kurd) The best or most that has been done.

segregated (SEH-gruh-gay-tid) When people of different races are separated.

scout (SKOWT) Someone who is paid to find talented athletes.

Index